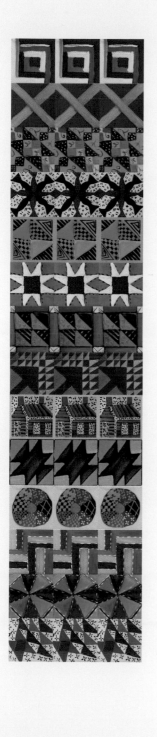

I Lay My Stitches Down

Poems of American Slavery

Written by
Cynthia Grady

Illustrated by
Michele Wood

Eerdmans Books for Young Readers
Grand Rapids, Michigan • Cambridge, U.K.

For Tylka, with love.
— *C. G.*

To my nieces, nephews, brother, and my future child.
Follow the light along the path of God because there will be precious jewels
to pick up on your way in life. The treasure will confirm the path you have taken is the right one.
I believe *I Lay My Stitches Down* is a gold nugget.
Follow the light.
— *M. W.*

Text © 2012 Cynthia Grady
Illustrations © 2012 Michele Wood

Published in 2012 by Eerdmans Books for Young Readers,
an imprint of Wm. B. Eerdmans Publishing Co.
2140 Oak Industrial Dr. NE
Grand Rapids, Michigan 49505
P.O. Box 163, Cambridge CB3 9PU U.K.

www.eerdmans.com/youngreaders

Manufactured at Tien Wah Press in Singapore in June 2011, first printing

12 13 14 15 16 17 18   9 8 7 6 5 4 3 2 1

Library of Congress Cataloging-in-Publication Data

Grady, Cynthia.
I lay my stitches down / by Cynthia Grady ; illustrated by Michele Wood.
p. cm.
ISBN 978-0-8028-5386-8 (alk. paper)
1. United States — History — Juvenile poetry. 2. United States — Biography — Juvenile poetry.
3. Children's poetry, American. [1. United States — History — Poetry. 2. American poetry.]
I. Wood, Michele, ill. II. Title.
PS3607.R3275I15 2012
811'.6 — dc23
2011022481

The illustrations were created with acrylics on canvas.
The display type was set in Casablanca Antique.
The text type was set in Adobe Garamond Pro.

Quiltmaking and poetry share similarities in craft. In one, color and shape are organized into an overall pattern; in the other, sound and structure create the pattern. Each poem in this collection is named for a traditional quilt block and reflects a metaphorical patchwork of circumstances encountered by enslaved people in America.

The poems are written in unrhymed verse, ten lines of ten syllables, to mimic the square shape of a quilt block. To reflect the three layers of a quilt, I've engaged three references in each poem: a biblical or spiritual reference, a musical reference, and a sewing or fiber arts reference in addition to the imagery the poem calls for. In this way I have tried to mirror not only the structure of a quilt but also the artistry and symbolism that quilts express for their makers.

— *Cynthia Grady*

Log Cabin

The finds of archaeologists beneath
dilapidated cabins down the hill:
some chicken bones, the skins and skulls of coons
and squirrels — hard remains of suppers stalked
by moonlight, faith, starvation. Caches, too,
of divination: sea shells, broken beads,
and bundled roots suggest how slaves survived
a knotted life of cornmeal, cruelty, death.
The dig won't yield the stolen, lost, withheld:
shoes, safety, drums, dignity, daughters, sons.

Archaeologists excavating the areas where enslaved Africans
and African Americans lived have discovered artifacts that
resemble ritual objects similar to those used in West African
religious practices. These artifacts have been found buried
in symbolic arrangements and clustered near doorways and
chimneys — thresholds for people and spirits.

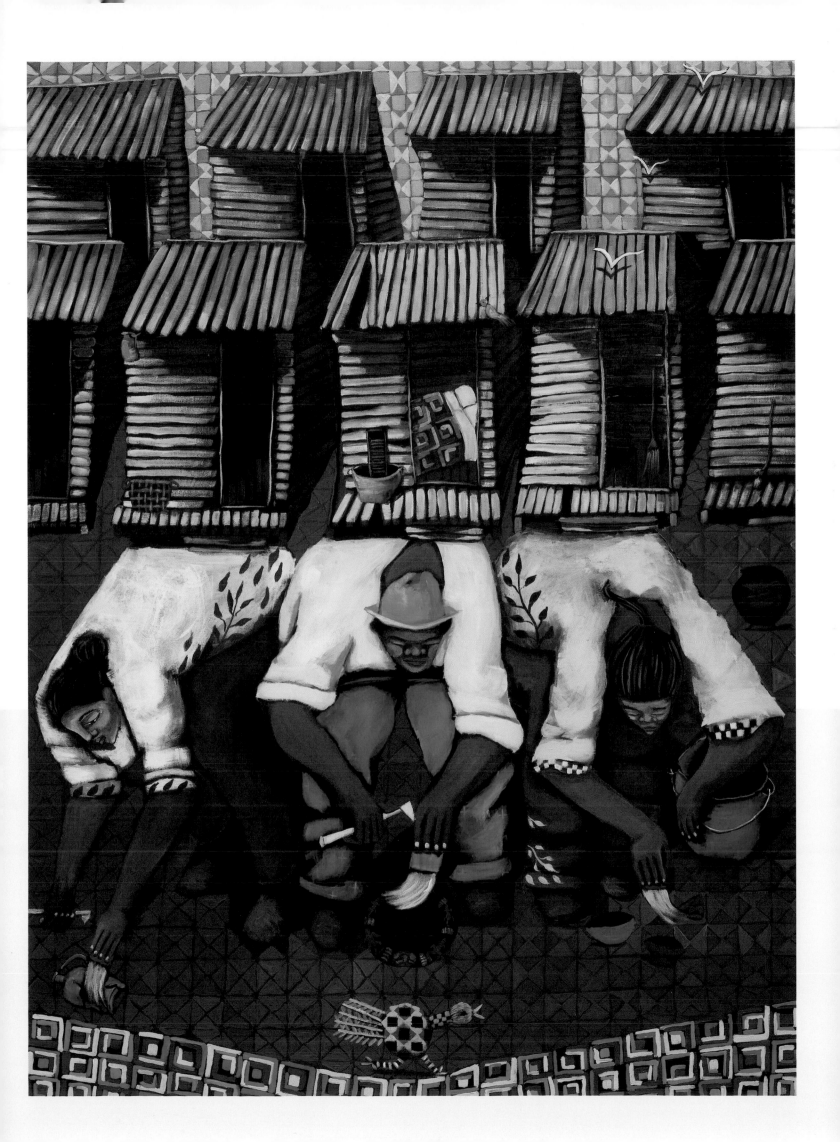

Cotton Boll

I need the music of my forebears from
Afrik, but take the mending to my lap
and work beside the Missus' chair. A spell
of quiet sewing, restful breath — it soothe
my soul, dangling by a thread that been spun
like cotton fiber grown and pinched on this
hell place. Before I know, I'm rocking with
the rhythm of the stitching, humming low
the melody of "Gilead." A balm
for hunger, sorrow, heartache, yes, he is.

A healing ointment found in Gilead on the eastern shore of the
Jordan River was so curative that it was equal in worth to salt,
a precious commodity in ancient times. In the Hebrew Bible,
or Old Testament, the prophet Jeremiah warns that not even
this balm's healing qualities are enough to rescue sinners from
God's judgment. Interestingly, the traditional spiritual "There
Is a Balm in Gilead" refers to Jesus of the New Testament, who
would heal all, regardless of their sins.

Underground Railroad

Like a hyena on the hunt, you know,
he opportunistic, unspecialized.
The bounty hunter prowl the riverbank.
He use the wind to his advantage and
he listen; he watch intently. A slave
to greed, the hunter aine no match for this
old pilgrim in the woods. He don't quite hear
the owl that call my name to take me to
the water where the current runs less swift.
I wait — then thread my way to freedomland.

Helping slaves escape to freedom through the network of people called the Underground Railroad was highly secretive, dangerous work that involved deception of all kinds — especially since slave owners often hired bounty hunters to track down runaway slaves. Using bird calls was one way for slaves to communicate with one another without being detected.

———

A pilgrim is a person of religious devotion who embarks on a spiritual journey. For some slaves, the quest for freedom was a spiritual journey as well as a physical one.

———

"Take Me to the Water" is the name of a spiritual referring to baptism by immersion in a river or lake. Here, the phrase also signifies crossing the Ohio River into safety.

Traditional Fish

Come August, Young Master and me runs through
the cool of the hick'ry nut grove to find
our friend canoeing downstream, smooth as a
needle through silk. We wade in, a-whistling,
beach his boat. Fish the old river with hand
spears — sharpened bone tied to wooden shaft — not
a pole and line. Aim low on account of
the trick the light play in shallow waters.
We thank Creation, church-like, for the catch,
and pray we three be best friends forever.

When enslaved children were still too young to work the fields, they spent their days playing after the morning chores of slopping hogs or milking cows, sweeping or gardening. They often played with children in the master's family. Before American Indians were "removed" to reservations by the U.S. government, they often lived near plantation communities in varying degrees of friendship and cooperation with slaves and slaveholders.

Broken Dishes

She always needling me. "Add some more salt."
Or, "Girl, why cain't you move faster than that?"
Her voice so shrill, it make your skin goose up.
I move fast, all right. A heap of gold-rimmed
plates brighter than the halo on the head
of Baby Jesus in one hand, platter
with green beans and collards in the other,
I done trip over the piano bench.
Lord, those flyin' plates look like angels, but
I 'spect tomorrow be the fields for me.

Working as a domestic slave had some advantages over field work. Often,
though not always, house slaves lived within the master's household
rather than in the slave cabins, so living conditions were better. But being
under the constant watchful eye of the master's family came with its own
set of problems. If the master and his wife were not particularly attached
to their house slaves, they would threaten the slaves with being sent to
work in the fields if their work or attitude was found unsatisfactory.

North Star

Age six saw me with a new master. He
was no slaver. Instead of tobacco
fields, I plowed the planes of Euclid. Instead
of flax, I spun my way through Homer's verse.
I longed to hear the heavenly hymns of
Pythagoras one starry night, when a
voice in the salt shed said, "Makes no diff'rence
what you know. A body wants to be free."
I bade my master farewell. His blessings
send me north, lighting my way to freedom.

Sometimes white people, whether they supported slavery or not, inherited slaves from relatives. What should they do? Should they raise the children as family members? Pay them for their work? Some educated their slaves privately, so that when they were freed, they could go into the world with knowledge and skills.

———

The writings of Euclid, Homer, and Pythagoras mentioned here were part of a classical education commonly taught in the nineteenth century.

———

The North Star shines directly above the North Pole and appears to be stationary, while the other stars revolve around the earth's axis as the earth rotates around the sun. Navigators have used the North Star for centuries to guide them in their travels. Slaves, too, used the North Star to navigate their way to freedom.

Birds in the Air

At morning's hush, when stars begin to fall,
she'll toss a pan of corn down behind the
quarters, whistling pure and sharp. Like the wren's
song, she hits the grace note just so. Soon, we
see wings aquiver; sky fills with birdsong.
Through a thick weave of Western clouds comes a
feathery carpet of birds. In makeshift
nests, they leave us their eggs. She makes her way
to the Big House to work, but not 'til we've
given thanks for her heavenly breakfast.

"When the stars begin to fall" is a line from a traditional spiritual called
"My Lord, What a Morning." For Christian slaves, morning was an
especially hopeful time. In the Bible, morning is the time of deliverance,
of ultimate victory over the injustices suffered during life on earth.

———

Slaves usually had to depend on food distributed by the master each
week for their meals, but this was rarely enough. Sometimes they were
allowed to keep chickens and a small garden, and they also found eggs
in the nests of stray or wild turkeys, geese, and ducks.

Tree of Life

Left tied to this tree, a patchwork of cuts
on fire across my back, I r'member
Preacher John, who come on moonless nights. He
a dark man. A free man. After preachin',
he say, "I'ma sit with you. Lean against
you, like the lashing tree that takes in your
cries, drinks your tears. I'ma hear your song that
stirs the soul like sap rising at winter's
end. Righteous melody that takes root where
you weep. Then sings through you blossoms of joy."

The "Tree of Life" quilt block pattern takes its name from the book of Genesis. In addition to fruit-bearing trees in the Garden of Eden, two trees are mentioned: the tree of life and the tree of the knowledge of good and evil.

Whipping was the most common form of punishment for slaves and could be carried out for a range of offenses, such as failing to work hard enough, fighting, stealing, or trying to run away.

In many regions, slaves were not allowed to worship without a white person present. Often slaves held secret worship services at night. In an attempt to muffle their voices, the worshipers would hang soaking wet blankets around them as they sang and shouted, or sometimes they would prop up iron pots and kettles to catch the sound.

Schoolhouse

Each morning after walking Little Miss
to school, we steal away beneath the oak
to piece together everything we hear.
The teacher catch us making letters in
the dirt with sticks one day. Her eyes go wide
and icy blue. She walk away. We fear'd
our backs would get the rawhide switch. Instead,
she twitch the curtain at the window, teach
her lessons loud and clear — her voice, a prayer
with wings. It give us hope; it sing us home.

In many states, slaves were forbidden to read and write. If a person were caught teaching a slave, both teacher and slave would be severely punished.

———

To "steal away" was a common expression that meant to sneak off, as if to hide. "Steal Away" is also the name of a spiritual that expresses the hope of escaping to a life of salvation.

Anvil

RRRRING! Ol' Pap, he a smith straight from Afrik.
He give the whites the blank stare. RRRRING! Massuh
think Pap don't speak English. CLANGGG!! Then Pap turn
his teasing eyes on me. CLONGGGG!! His blue-black,
braided arms lift the hammer; it fall to
release a musical spill of sparks. PINNGGG!
He quench the hinge, HISSSsssssss, in a bucket. 'Fore
Pap transform his next chunk of iron, he
chant a prayer, then work the bellows, WWHooooSHH, to
kindle the fire, the embers of his faith.

A blacksmith heats iron in a fire until it is soft enough to mold with his hammers and other tools. The smooth, steel-faced iron block upon which the smith works is called the anvil.

———

In some African mythologies the divine smith is the inventor of fire, and the transformation of metals through the use of fire is considered a divine act. All blacksmiths were thought to be descendants of and apprentices to the divine smith.

Wagon Wheel

That overseer cut from the same cloth
as the devil hisself, the very warp
and weft. When he come to the cabins, Lord
have mercy, a wagonload of sadness
ain't far behind; someone 'bout to be sold.
This morn he come for my baby girl — she
done reach her breeding age. Fetch a good price.
Her mama moaning low, long burying
songs; greedy wheels groaning, drag my heart clean
out of my chest, leaving only the grief.

Slaveholders sold their slaves at auction for many reasons: to pay off debts,
to increase wealth, and sometimes to punish a slave. Strong men, as well as
women of child-bearing age, brought the highest prices. Keeping families
together was usually not important to slave owners, and many slaves lost
family members to auction.

———

When cloth is woven on a loom, the vertical threads are called the "warp"
threads and the horizontal threads are called "weft." The expression "cut from
the same cloth" means two people are very similar to one another.

Rail Fence

White man's devil trots on a horse's hoof.
The stallion rears, then bucks, whinnies, stomps, and
snorts. Runs in cock-eyed circles to draw my
rage. But I know horses. Ev'ry earflick,
hoof, and muscle. I catch the light of fear
in his eyes. Smooth my right hand 'cross his chest.
He knickers, blows. In moments we're walking
the same path, leading, being led, from discord into harmony, within this fenced
paradise, this patchwork field of freedom.

In the early days of horse racing in the South, the horses were
groomed, exercised, trained, and raced by slaves. Africans and African
Americans dominated the sport until the late 1800s.

———

"Discord" is a clash of sounds. In music, when clashing notes move
into harmony, they form a tuneful sound that works as a whole, just
as this trainer and his new horse do.

Kaleidoscope

The little time we have to call our own
be filled with gardening, feeding chickens,
mending clothes, and music-making: shaking
stones in a basket, clapping hands, stomping
feet. Sometimes a banjo and fiddle be
played, or hollowed-out tree drum and washboard.
But lo, the singing! Piecing shouts here to
Bible stories there, interweaving tunes
and hollers, singing up a frenzy of
song! Be a kaleidoscope of sound: Joy.

Most slaves worked for their masters from before sunup until after
sundown, six, sometimes seven, days a week. Many masters, however,
allowed a break for their slaves on Saturday nights or Sundays. A few
festivals and frolics might be held throughout the year as well: Fourth
of July, Christmas, corn-shucking, wheat-threshing, and syrup-cooking
time. Sometimes even quiltings included music and dancing for those
who didn't sew.

Basket

Each night I take my patches, blocks, and scraps
of fabric from the basket by the chair;
my thimble, thread, and needle comfort me.
I lay my stitches down and troubles fall
away. Before too long, I'm breathing with
the rhythm of my quilting — listening
wide with every fiber of my soul:
the praise songs of my people; voices of
my kin; drumbeats of my motherland form
the threads that weave the fabric of my life.

Large work baskets woven from a marsh grass called bulrush were made by slaves and used for gathering and storing rice and vegetables as well as cotton, shellfish, and grain. Smaller baskets were made from the more pliable sweetgrasses for bread and sewing storage. Basket-making is one of the oldest art forms of West African origin still practiced in the United States.

Many of the world's religious traditions — Judaism, Christianity, Islam, Zen Buddhism, and others — implore us to be quiet, to listen. The book of Isaiah tells us, "Hear and your soul shall live."

Author's Note

A few years ago over a winter holiday, I made preparations to teach a quilting class to a small group of middle schoolers. I wanted to teach quilt blocks that would be easy for beginners to piece together, and I wanted blocks with provocative names that we could talk about while we worked. The first block I put to graph paper was "Underground Railroad."

I measured and outlined and then began to fill in the design with colored pencils. As I worked, the first three poems, all concerning slavery, came as a gift, all at once. I had to stop drafting my pattern to write the poems down.

I was so intrigued by this experience that I began researching American slavery and quilt history. I read letters, diaries, speeches, and sermons. I read fiction and poetry. I listened to as much music as I could find, beginning with the earliest recordings of music created by Africans and African Americans in this country. I spoke with quilt historians and museum curators. The remaining poems evolved slowly over the next year. I am indebted to my quilting teachers and writing mentors, past and present, especially Mary Quattlebaum and Sandra Duncan, for their help during this process.

While quilt historians and American history experts may disagree on the subject, legends surrounding slaves and their use of quilts to escape to freedom persist. This book does not attempt to enter the historical controversy but, rather, gives voice to distinct characters, bound together by the common thread of prevailing laws and prejudices of the time.

— *Cynthia Grady*

Illustrator's Note

I felt drawn to this book from the moment I read the first poem. The language in these poems spoke to my spirit, encouraging me as each painting complemented Cynthia's strong, beautifully expressed stories. I am fascinated by the spirit of enslaved people — especially their tremendous faith and their strength to endure. Because of their endurance and determination to survive, a new breed of Americans emerged.

I have been researching American and African history for many years. I have traveled the southern region of the United States, lived among southern people, and interviewed southerners and members of my own family in order to capture the essence of the South in my art. For instance, I painted a mule in the "Basket" illustration because a friend from Louisiana who grew up picking cotton told me that people in the South who were too poor to own an ox plowed with mules instead. In addition to reading extensively on the subjects covered in this book, I have drawn upon my own travel to Africa and my personal knowledge of Christianity in order to express the spirit, wisdom, and bravery of the people depicted here. I concentrated especially on African and American textiles to convey the complex, rich culture of African American slaves.

— *Michele Wood*

For Further Reading

Brackman, Barbara. *Facts and Fabrications: Unraveling the History of Quilts and Slavery*. Lafayette, CA: C & T Publications, 2006.

Fradin, Dennis Brindell. *Bound for the North Star: True Stories of Fugitive Slaves*. New York: Clarion, 2000.

Hamilton, Virginia. *Many Thousands Gone: African Americans from Slavery to Freedom*. Illustrated by Leo Dillon and Diane Dillon. New York: Knopf, 1993.

Haskins, James, and Kathleen Benson. *Building a New Land: African Americans in Colonial America*. Illustrated by James Ransome. New York: HarperCollins, 2001.

McGill, Alice. *In the Hollow of Your Hand: Slave Lullabies*. Illustrated by Michael Cummings. New York: Houghton Mifflin, 2000.

McKissack, Patricia C., and Frederick L. McKissack. *Days of Jubilee: The End of Slavery in the United States*. Illustrated by Leo Dillon and Diane Dillon. New York: Scholastic, 2003.

Osborne, Linda Barrett. *Traveling the Freedom Road: From Slavery and the Civil War through Reconstruction*. New York: Abrams, 2009.

Taylor, Yuval, ed. *Growing Up in Slavery: Stories of Young Slaves as Told by Themselves*. Chicago: Lawrence Hill Books, 2005.

Waldstreicher, David. *The Struggle Against Slavery: A History in Documents*. New York: Oxford, 2001.

Warren, Gwendolyn Sims. *Ev'ry Time I Feel the Spirit: 101 Best-Loved Psalms, Gospel Hymns, and Spiritual Songs of the African-American Church*. New York: Henry Holt, 1997.

White, Shane, and Graham White. *The Sounds of Slavery: Discovering African American History through Songs, Sermons, and Speech*. Boston: Beacon Press, 2005.